Wrestling
Greats

BRET HART

Ross Davies

The Rosen Publishing Group, Inc.
New York

Published in 2002 by The Rosen Publishing Group, Inc.
29 East 21st Street, New York, NY 10010

Copyright © 2002 by The Rosen Publishing Group, Inc.

First Edition

Library of Congress Cataloging-in-Publication Data

Davies, Ross.
Bret Hart / by Ross Davies. — 1st ed.
p. cm. — (Wrestling greats)
Includes bibliographical references (p.) and index.
ISBN 0-8239-3494-2
1. Hart, Bret—Juvenile literature. 2. Wrestlers—Canada—
Biography—Juvenile literature. [1. Hart, Bret. 2. Wrestlers.]
I. Title. II. Series
GV1196.H33 D38 2001
796.812'092—dc21

2001001519

Manufactured in the United States of America

Contents

Bret Hart was a WCW wrestler, a five-time WWF world champion, and one-half of the legendary tag team, the Hart Foundation.

One for Owen

On November 21, 1999, Bret Hart suspected that he had reached his final moment of truth. Forty-two years of life had brought him to this point: standing in the middle of the ring at the Air Canada Centre in Toronto. Forty-two years. Five World Wrestling Foundation world heavyweight championships. The deaths of two brothers, one almost exactly six months earlier. Forty-two years of pride and heart and soul had brought the Hitman to this point—a chance to win his first World Championship Wrestling (WCW) world heavyweight title.

Chris Benoit, the Canadian Crippler, wasn't his only opponent.

"I wasn't really worried about winning or losing," Bret Hart wrote in his *Calgary Sun* column the following week. "I just wanted to be able to look at myself in the mirror and know that Owen would have been proud . . . I could feel Owen watching—as if he'd pulled up a chair, like a fan, eager to see something special from me and Chris. Something we hadn't seen on TV for too long a time. 'Dungeon' wrestling. A straight-forward, shoot-from-the-hip wrestling match. Artistry at its best."

Hart had always been an artist in the ring, a man who cared about his craft. Now, in the finals of a thirty-two-man tournament for the vacant world title, he and the rest of the world would find out if he had the intestinal fortitude to recover from the death of his beloved brother, Owen, and once again be the best there is, the best there was, and the best there ever would be.

Earlier in the evening, Hart had beaten Sting in the semifinals of the tournament. Benoit had beaten Jeff Jarrett. Hart and Benoit had wrestled several times before, but never with so much at stake. Fans held up signs urging Bret Hart to "Do It for Owen," and Hart, who had always considered himself the "Excellence of Execution," intended to do just that.

The bell rang. Hart caught Benoit in his sharpshooter, a variation of the figure-four leglock. Benoit escaped and caught Hart in a Crippler crossface. Benoit scored with a suplex and a flying headbutt, but Dean Malenko interfered and attacked Benoit with a chair. Security took Malenko away and the match continued until Scott Hall and Kevin Nash interfered, too. They pulled the referee out of the ring, knocked him out, then climbed into the ring and attacked both Hart and Benoit. The heavyweight title match had turned into a free-for-all.

Fortunately, former world champion Bill Goldberg stormed the ring and chased off Hall and Nash. The match continued. Hart clotheslined Benoit and sent him careening over the top rope. Then he suplexed Benoit back into the ring. With seventeen minutes gone in the match, Benoit battled back and caught Hart in the Crippler crossface. Hart broke the hold by elbowing Benoit in the stomach, then turned, dropped Benoit to the mat, and locked on his sharp-shooter, which is his finishing move. Seconds later, Benoit submitted. Hart had managed to win his first WCW world championship.

Bret Hart dedicated his WCW world championship title to the memory of his brother, Owen, who gave his life to wrestling, the sport they both loved.

The crowd exploded with excitement. Bret Hart's wife, Julie, and their four children cheered in celebration. Benoit graciously shook hands with Hart, who grabbed a Canadian flag and waved it around the ring. The crowd's cheers got louder.

"This is a special night for me," Hart said later. "I came to WCW to prove that I am the best there is, the best there was, and the best there ever will be. And it was an honor to do it in front of the fans of Canada."

He had done it for Canada, his native country. He had done it for himself. But most of all, Bret Hart had won for Owen, whose death he would forever mourn. Glory had been taken from Bret Hart before. This time, it would be his forever.

2 The Reluctant Wrestler

The story of the Hart wrestling family begins in 1915, when Stu Hart (Bret's father), was born in a small town outside Edmonton, Alberta. Life wasn't easy for the Harts. The family lived in a tent, and Stu's father hunted for food in the wilderness. From this rugged background, one of the toughest men in wrestling history was created.

At an early age, Stu took up wrestling at the local YMCA, where the bigger, stronger wrestlers frequently humiliated him. Regardless, Stu never quit. He considered the taunting as a lesson in pain, and he kept on wrestling

His hard work and determination paid off. He became an outstanding amateur wrestler and a member of the Canadian national team. Stu won a Canadian amateur wrestling championship and played a year in the Canadian Football League with the Edmonton Eskimos. But wrestling was his true calling. After World War II, Stu moved to New York City to become a pro wrestler.

Stu met Helen, who would become his wife. They bought a twenty-one-room house, a former army hospital near Calgary. About a year after buying the house, Stu transformed the basement into a personal training center—called the Dungeon—with weights, wrestling mats, and other apparatus. By the early 1950s, Stu had made enough money wrestling that he was able to open his own company, called Stampede Wrestling, in Calgary.

Helen was Stu's business partner. They had twelve children together: eight boys and four girls. All eight boys would follow their father into pro wrestling. All four girls would marry professional wrestlers. Smith was the first of the eight

Hart boys, followed by Bruce, Keith, Wayne, and Dean. Next came Bret and after him came Ross and Owen.

Bret Hart was born on July 2, 1957. If the first sounds he ever heard were those of his mother and father and the doctor who delivered him, the next sounds he heard were the screams of pain coming from the Dungeon. Even though the Dungeon was originally conceived as a training center for Stu and other pro wrestlers, it quickly became training grounds for the Hart boys. Stu was a tough taskmaster. He taught his students to withstand almost unbearable pain.

"I can remember my dad squeezing me so hard that the blood vessels would

Bret Hart takes a breather
on the ropes during a bout.

break behind my eyeballs and I'd go to school the next day with red eyes," Bret Hart said in *Hitman Hart: Wrestling with Shadows*, a documentary that aired on television on the A&E Network.

By the time he was four-and-a-half years old, Bret was already working for his father, selling programs for the wrestling cards at the Stampede Pavilion. Bret also set up the ring and played the music that accompanied the wrestlers' entrances.

Growing up, Bret was surrounded by wrestlers. Many times, wrestlers who were in town for a card at the Stampede Pavilion would drop by the Hart house for dinner, and would then enjoy some after-dinner entertainment in the Dungeon.

Abdullah the Butcher and Archie the Stomper, who were both trained by Stu, were regular guests. However, Helen didn't want her children to become wrestlers, and she cringed whenever her husband's after-dinner demonstrations were performed with the children as the victims.

Bret attended Wildwood Elementary School in Calgary, where life wasn't always easy. Sometimes he had to defend himself from kids who would say that both wrestling and his dad were fakes. And of course, Bret felt obligated to defend himself and his father. "As a kid, I thought I couldn't lose," Bret said in his autobiography, *Bret "Hitman" Hart.* "It was impossible. You were supposed to win."

That pressure came from being the son of a father who was used to winning. Stu expected nothing but the best from his children. He taught them how to win and how to be tough. However, he also taught them discipline, integrity, and respect.

When Bret joined the wrestling club at the local YMCA, and then started wrestling competitively in junior high school, he did it only to impress his father. In eleventh grade, Bret won the city championship, but lost the provincial championship after breaking his collar-bone. The next year, Bret won both the city championship and the Alberta provincial championship.

Regardless of his success, Bret wasn't sure that he wanted to be a pro wrestler. The fact of the matter was that he wanted to be a movie director. Bret idolized director Martin Scorcese. Although Bret had mastered the fundamentals of pro wrestling and was a great wrestler at Ernest Manning High School in Calgary, he planned to go in a completely different direction after graduating.

Growing up, Bret was surrounded by wrestlers.

Bret took a year and a half off after high school graduation and worked at a gas plant to pay for his tuition at Mount Royal College in Calgary. While fighting off pressure from family and friends to go into pro wrestling, Bret took a year of broadcasting classes at Mount Royal. However, he didn't do very well. Aside from his classes, Bret wrestled for the college team and at night he refereed matches for his father. Bret didn't have a lot of time to study. Often, he skipped classes entirely.

After dropping out of college, Bret continued to work as a referee for Stu. He went all over western Canada, but made only minimum wage. It was during this time that Bret realized that he could wrestle better than his father's wrestlers. Stampede Wrestling tag team champs Mr. Hito and Mr. Sakarada convinced Bret to let them train him in the Dungeon. For months, the Japanese stars put Bret through grueling training sessions. Finally, in 1976, Bret filled in for a wrestler on one of his father's cards. His opponents in the tag team match were Hito and Sakarada.

"They kicked the crap out of me," Bret recalled. "I thought they might take it easy but they really hurt me. I remember almost having tears in my eyes. They told me they had no choice, that it was all part of paying my dues."

For the rest of that night, Bret was wracked with aches and pains, but when he woke up the next morning, Bret Hart was certain of his future: He was going to be a professional wrestler.

3 You Gotta Have Hart

There was no reason for Bret Hart to leave Calgary. Aside from his job with Stampede Wrestling, his family and his friends were there. It was there that Hart would meet his future wife, Julie, in the late 1970s. Hart and Julie married in 1980.

It was truly a family affair. With both Stampede Wrestling and the Puerto Rico–based World Wrestling Council, Bret often teamed with two of his brothers, Smith and Keith. The brothers won several tag team championships in both areas. Bret tasted singles glory for the first time in 1978, when he won the British Commonwealth mid-heavyweight title.

Hart's numerous battles for the British Commonwealth throne took on an interesting flavor because he was wrestling against his own family members. His main rival for the title was Davey Boy Smith, who, like Hart, was a talented mat wrestler. But Davey Boy would one day marry Hart's sister, Diana, and Hart would later engage in tag team and singles feuds with Davey Boy in the World Wrestling Federation (WWF).

Hart was fabulously successful during his six years in Calgary. He won six North American heavyweight titles and fought some exciting matches against Harley Race, the former National Wrestling Alliance world champion. In Japan, Hart beat Ted DiBiase to win the International Wrestling Grand Prix title. Hart also wrestled in Germany and England. He also feuded with Jim Neidhart, his future tag team partner.

The fans in Calgary, who loved the Hart brothers, had no doubt that when they were watching Hart wrestle, they were witnessing a star in the making. Hart, however, had one shortcoming: He was extremely shy and reserved, and he didn't like doing television interviews. Of course, television interviews are an important part of wrestling; they are as vital to a wrestler's image and public persona as what the wrestler accomplishes in the ring.

To compensate for his shyness, Hart began to create a new persona for himself. First, Hart thought up a nickname: the Hitman. The name came from boxer Tommy "the Hitman" Hearns, whom Hart admired. Then Hart started wearing dark wraparound sunglasses decorated with colorful flames. This helped to hide his nervousness during interviews. Ultimately, the nickname and the glasses became Hart's trademarks.

Early in his career, Bret Hart assumed the nickname the Hitman.
The name and his dark sunglasses became his trademarks.

Things were going well for Hart. His career was progressing nicely. He and Julie had their first of four children. Then he got his big break. In 1984, with Stampede attendance down, Stu Hart sold the federation to Vince McMahon Jr., owner of the WWF. The deal made Bret Hart a member of the most successful wrestling federation in North America.

There was only one problem: Bret wasn't really cut out for the WWF. Hulk Hogan had recently won the WWF world heavyweight title, and Hulkamania was running wild in North America. Hulkamania meant flashy outfits, loud music, and wrestlers who stormed into the ring, attacked their opponents, and ended their matches as quickly as possible by kicking and punching. Hart, who wasn't flashy and preferred wearing down his opponents methodically, was the opposite of what Hulkamania represented.

"My first match in the WWF was in Hamilton, Ontario [against the Dynamite Kid], and it always reminds me of that big hook on Broadway they used to pull the crappy entertainers off the stage," Hart told the *Calgary Sun*. "Vince said 'that Dynamite Kid is great and Bret is horrible.' After that, I couldn't get a break."

Things got worse before they got better. Around the middle of 1984, Hart underwent surgery on his injured right knee. He recovered fully, toured Japan for five weeks, then flew back to Calgary and wrestled mostly in the western provinces. His matches were frequently the first on a card; in other words, he wrestled when most of the fans were still settling into their seats.

It was during this period that Hart started to become frustrated. He knew in his heart that he was a better wrestler than Hogan and most of the other WWF wrestlers. He knew that he worked harder than anyone, but nobody seemed to notice his mat skills. Hart would have been very popular in the 1950s and 1960s, when wrestling skill was considered important. Unfortunately, in the new age of rock 'n' wrestling, Bret Hart was boring.

Shortly thereafter, Hart came up with an idea. He thought that he and Jim Neidhart, against whom he had previously wrestled, could make a strong rulebreaking tag team. He figured that Neidhart's toughness would be the perfect compliment to his mat skills. Hart was on the verge of quitting in March 1985 when he called the WWF and said, "Put me and Neidhart together."

To his surprise, the WWF said OK. Jimmy Hart, the loudmouth manager who wore colorful suits and brought a bullhorn to the ring, would compliment the duo. The Hart Foundation was born.

The Hitman, the Anvil, and the Mouth of the South

A person who has a vibrant personality is said to have "color." In the opinion of WWF fans and executives, Bret Hart and Jim Neidhart didn't have any color. Most of the duo's personality came from their manager, Jimmy "the Mouth of the South" Hart.

In the fall of 1986, at a card in San Diego, Bret Hart and Neidhart made an effort to rectify their "colorless" situation:

The Hart Foundation introduced its new wrestling outfits—hot pink tights with black and pink tank tops. As Hart recalled in his autobiography, Vince McMahon couldn't believe what he was seeing.

"He walked around us and said, 'Don't ever change this color. This is you. This is your color from now on,' " Hart recalled in an interview." 'This is the one thing you guys have been missing since you've been here. You've had no color. Now you have color.' "

Jimmy Hart said in a WWF video interview, "These guys are the only guys bad enough to walk down the streets of any city in the world and wear pink and get away with it."

That was the whole idea: The Hart Foundation was mean enough, tough enough, and good enough to wear any color it wanted. Even pink.

The Hart Foundation was on its way to superstardom. When the British Bulldogs, the team of Davey Boy Smith and Dynamite Kid, won the WWF world tag team title at WrestleMania II, Hart and Neidhart set their sights on winning the championship.

The Bulldogs and the Harts had a spectacular feud. While the rest of the WWF wrestlers were brawling, the Harts and the Bulldogs were showing off both the beauty and brutality of wrestling. Of course, when the going got tough for

Bret Hart went from being a "colorless" unknown to having plenty of color—and fame—with the Hart Foundation.

the Harts, the Mouth of the South was always there to interfere.

The Hart Foundation won its first world tag team title by beating the Bulldogs on January 26, 1987, in Tampa, Florida. The match was marred by the controversial interference of referee Danny Davis, who had been bribed by Jimmy Hart. At WrestleMania III, Davis teamed with Bret Hart and Neidhart against the Bulldogs and Tito Santana. Davis grabbed Jimmy Hart's megaphone, slugged Davey Boy, and scored the pin.

The Hart Foundation was on a roll. If Jimmy Hart wasn't cheating on the team's behalf, then Davis was. They quickly became the most hated tag team in the federation. Bret Hart enjoyed the role of rulebreaker. He strutted and bragged about the team's greatness . . . even after the Hart Foundation lost the belts to Strike Force on October 27, 1987, in Syracuse, New York. Hart had reason to brag: *Pro Wrestling Illustrated* magazine named the Hart Foundation runners-up for Tag Team of the Year.

Despite the Hart Foundation's rule-breaking antics, fans who were paying attention couldn't deny that Hart was a great wrestler. Hart's performance at the 1988 Royal Rumble was eye-catching. In the Royal Rumble, wrestlers enter the ring one by one and are eliminated one by one. The last man standing is the winner.

The Rumble is a test of stamina, and Hart passed the test. Although he didn't win, he lasted thirty-six minutes in the ring— more than any other wrestler—and eliminated several opponents.

Things started to change for Hart at WrestleMania IV on March 27, 1988, in Atlantic City, New Jersey. An attack by Bad News Brown started Hart's conversion from rulebreaker to fan favorite. The fans started rooting for Neidhart, too. Unfortunately, Jimmy Hart didn't want to be converted, and he was fired by the wrestlers. That started a long feud between the Hart Foundation and their former manager, who would go on to manage two of the Harts' main rivals: Demolition and the Rougeau

Brothers. For most of the next two years, the Hart Foundation concentrated on destroying the Mouth of the South and his teams.

Wrestling is all about winning titles, and the Hart Foundation won another one by beating Demolition on August 27, 1990, in Philadelphia. Their greatest title defense took place on October 30, 1990, when they took on the Rockers, the team of Marty Jannetty and Shawn Michaels. Like the Harts, the Rockers were fan favorites. The Rockers won the first fall of the best-of-three-falls match when Jannetty pinned Hart. In the second fall, Hart clotheslined Michaels and scored the pin. Earlier in the fall, however, the top rope had been knocked loose, causing the ropes to sag. In the third fall, Jannetty pinned Hart. The Rockers had apparently won the world tag team championship.

A day later, WWF president Jack Tunney overturned the Rockers' victory due to the sagging ropes. Hart and Neidhart had narrowly retained the world title.

This was a time of upheaval and sadness for Bret Hart. On November 21, 1990, his older brother, Dean, died of kidney disease. Bret was extremely distraught. As for the Hart Foundation, it had lost its magic. Hart and Neidhart realized that they had been lucky to get the belts back after the match against the Rockers. Perhaps it was time for a change.

Ultimately, the Hart Foundation lost the world tag team belts to the Nasty Boys (managed by Jimmy Hart) at WrestleMania VII. Brian Knobs pinned Hart to end their second reign as champions. After the loss, Hart and Neidhart decided to split up. The split was amicable. They both had new goals and aspirations. Their time together had been fruitful. Hart and Neidhart were now stars.

Bret Hart was about to become the biggest star of all.

Getting By on His Own

Could a man really change so much in only five years? After all, as early as 1985, Bret Hart had failed in his attempt to become a successful singles wrestler in the WWF. Most wrestling fans saw Hart as a tag team wrestler. They were unaware of his numerous singles titles in western Canada, and had forgotten his great run at the 1988 Royal Rumble. Could Bret Hart survive without Jim Neidhart? That was the question on the minds of many people.

Hart had no doubt that he would not only survive, but thrive. He wasted no time proving himself right. He piled up decisive pinfall victories over mid-level wrestlers such as the Barbarian, Irwin R. Schyster, Dino Bravo, and the Warlord.

That positioned Hart for a series of matches against WWF intercontinental champion, Curt Hennig. The intercontinental is considered the WWF's secondary title, just one step down from the world title, and is one of the most prestigious in wrestling. Such great stars as Pedro Morales, Greg Valentine, Randy Savage, the Ultimate Warrior, Rick Rude, Diesel (Kevin Nash), Shawn Michaels, Steve Austin, Triple-H, and the Rock have tasted I-C title glory.

Unfortunately, Hart's first few runs at the intercontinental title were unsuccessful. Hennig was an intelligent, wily wrestler who, like Hart, knew his way around the ring and had a wide repertoire of scientific and amateur moves. Hennig lost several title defenses to Hart, but retained the championship by countout. According to WWF rules, a title can only change hands if the champion is pinned or submits.

Hart and Hennig met again at SummerSlam '91 on August 26, 1991, at Madison Square Garden in New York. A sellout crowd, including Stu, Helen, and Bruce Hart, packed this famous arena. Although Randy Savage's marriage to his manager, Elizabeth, was the main event of

SummerSlam '91, Hart and Hennig did their best to steal the show.

Moments after the opening bell, Hart connected with a shoulder block, then hip-tossed Hennig out of the ring. Hennig had come into the match with an injured back, and Hart spent most of the match concentrating on his opponent's physical weakness. Hart got one near-pinfall after another, but couldn't score the finishing pin. When he prevented Hennig from fleeing to the locker room, the intercontinental champion got down to business. He caught Hart in a sleeperhold, a move which restricts the flow of blood to the brain and causes the victim to pass out. Hart narrowly fought his way out of the hold.

Hart realized that he was in the match of his life. If he lost to Hennig, there was a chance he'd never get another shot at the title. If he won, he'd be one step closer to being on top of the wrestling world. As the match continued, and Hennig's dominance became unquestionable, Hart recalled his time spent in the Dungeon. He remembered the lessons his father (who was sitting at ringside) had taught him about being tough, digging down deep for something extra, and never giving in. He remembered the punishment he had endured at the hands of his Japanese instructors.

Suddenly, in Hart's mind, he and Hennig were no longer in Madison Square Garden. They were in the Dungeon.

Bret Hart slams an opponent down on the mat.

Hart somehow summoned up an energy source he didn't even know existed. He scored with a vertical suplex, a small package, a neckbreaker, and a flying axhandle to get a series of two-counts. With Hennig on the mat and sufficiently weakened, Hart applied the sharpshooter. But Hennig's manager, John Tolos, climbed onto the ring apron. Hart released the sharpshooter and chased off Tolos.

Now Hart was down on the mat and Hennig moved in for the kill. He took his time, then soared into the air for a legdrop. Hart moved out of the way. Hennig crashed to the mat. Hart quickly moved into position and applied another sharpshooter. Hennig screamed out in pain and submitted.

Bret "the Hitman" Hart was the WWF intercontinental champion! He had proven to everyone that he could make it as a singles wrestler.

After the Hitman's victory, his opponents were intimidated by the sharpshooter. Although Hart seemed to be a little premature when he declared himself "the best there ever was, the best there is, and the best there ever will be," many people considered him the best wrestler in the WWF, better even than Hulk Hogan.

But there were setbacks. On January 17, 1992, Hart had a high fever and was suffering from the flu when he stepped into the ring for his match against the Mountie, in Springfield, Massachusetts. Hart could have backed out of the match, but he didn't expect the Mountie to be that much competition. One night, Hart had beat the Mountie in three seconds. Besides, the Mountie was managed by Jimmy Hart, and the Hitman never backed away from a challenge by Jimmy Hart.

The Hitman shouldn't have been so proud. That night, the Mountie beat him for the intercontinental title.

However, the Mountie's I-C title reign didn't last long. Two days later, he lost the belt to Roddy Piper, Bret Hart's longtime friend. That set up a match between Hart and Piper at WrestleMania VII on April 5 at the Hoosier Dome in Indianapolis, Indiana.

In one of the most intense matches ever fought, Bret countered Piper's sleeper by flipping him backwards to the mat, and then scoring the pin to retain the title.

Hart's second intercontinental title reign was even more impressive than the first. He defeated several top wrestlers, including rising singles star Shawn Michaels. But his ultimate test came at SummerSlam '92 at Wembley Stadium in London, England. His opponent was Davey Boy Smith, former member of the British Bulldogs, and now his brother-in-law.

Davey Boy, who was born in Leeds, England, was the clear hometown favorite, and he carried the fans' backing to a stunning victory. Months later, the match would be named Match of the Year by *Pro Wrestling Illustrated*, but that hardly mattered to Hart, who had lost the intercontinental title.

Fortunately for the Hart family, Bret and Davey Boy embraced after the match. Diana Smith climbed into the ring and celebrated with her husband and brother. Clearly, there were no hard feelings between the two combatants.

Besides, Bret Hart was ready for a bigger challenge.

The Best There Is

Ever since 1980, one wrestler has stood above all others as the standard by which technical wrestlers must be judged. If you want to be a brawler, you're measured against Hulk Hogan. But if you want to be a scientific wrestler who treats every match as a puzzle to be solved, you're measured against Ric Flair.

Flair arrived in the WWF in 1991 after spending most of his career in the National Wrestling Alliance (now known as World Championship Wrestling, or WCW). By the time Hart set his sights on the world title, Flair was a two-time WWF world champion. Hart really wanted to wrestle Flair, who was known as Nature Boy. He knew that to be the best there is, the best there was, and the best there ever will be, he'd have to beat the man who many considered the best there was.

After failing to beat Flair in several matches, Hart got the break he needed on October 12, 1992, when he had the home-mat advantage in a match against Flair in Saskatoon, Saskatchewan.

Flair versus Hart was actually a battle of similar submission holds: Hart's sharpshooter against Flair's figure-four leglock, the original version of Hart's sharpshooter. The match would come down to which man could force the other to submit to his signature move. Early in the match, Hart escaped Flair's figure-four. Few wrestlers had ever escaped the move. Flair maintained his advantage, but Hart kept reversing figure-fours. Finally, with twenty-five minutes into the match, Hart locked on his sharpshooter. Flair couldn't escape. Hart was WWF world champion for the first time.

"This is the greatest day of my life," Hart told a crowd of supporters. "I've got a lot to be thankful for, and I am proud to be

WWF champion. This is an example of hard work and perseverance paying off. I have been working toward this since I was a kid, and now I have reached the pinnacle of my career."

Hart had become the first person to win the WWF world, intercontinental, and world tag team titles. Now, when he called himself the best there ever was, he had solid evidence to back his claim.

Next, the Hitman embarked on an ambitious series of successful title defenses against Flair, Shawn Michaels, Ted DiBiase, Bam Bam Bigelow, and Razor Ramon. But his biggest challenge came in the form of 500-pound Yokozuna at WrestleMania IX in Las Vegas.

After an already illustrious career, Hart reached the top when he beat
Ric Flair for the WWF world title.

Hart had already beaten the former Sumo wrestler several times, but he was wary of Mr. Fuji, Yokozuna's manager, at WrestleMania IX. Hart had reason to be wary. Yokozuna was about to submit to Hart's sharpshooter when Mr. Fuji climbed onto the ring apron, took a handful of salt, and threw it in Hart's eyes. Hart flew back in pain and released the grip. Yokozuna splashed Hart and scored the pin. The Hitman's reign as WWF world champion was over.

Yokozuna's brief reign was about to end, too. Hogan ran out of the dressing room to argue with the referee and Mr. Fuji issued an impromptu challenge to the Hulkster. Hogan accepted and needed less than thirty seconds to pin Yokozuna.

Hart was enraged. He was angry at Mr. Fuji for cheating, at referee Earl Hebner for not catching Mr. Fuji in the act, and at Hogan for accepting Fuji's challenge. Weeks later, he was mad at Hogan for not giving him the first title shot. Not only did Hogan not offer Hart the first title shot, he never offered him any title shot.

A victory by Hart in the 1993 King of the Ring tournament incurred the wrath of Jerry "the King" Lawler, who considered himself to be the King of the Ring.

Over the following months, Lawler targeted Hart and his family with insults. He attacked Hart at every opportunity. Lawler so enraged Hart that one night, the Hitman refused to release his sharpshooter even after the referee had awarded him the victory. Fans were seeing the ruthless side of Bret Hart.

"Why do those guys always have to get in the way? I never get any recognition!"

-Owen Hart asked his father

At Survivor Series '93, Hart teamed up with his brothers Owen, Keith, and Bruce, in an elimination match against Shawn Michaels, the Black Knight, the Red Knight, and the Blue Knight. The Knights were all masked wrestlers Lawler had hired to do his dirty work for him.

Bret Hart was looking forward to the match and Thanksgiving dinner with his family the day after the Survivor Series. As it turned out, the match was a nightmare not only for Bret, but for Stu and Helen Hart, who were sitting ringside. Owen mistakenly struck Bret, and then was pinned by Michaels. As Keith and Bruce tended to Bret, who had struck the metal barrier that separates the crowd from the ring, Owen leaned over the ropes and yelled, "What about me?" Owen walked back to the dressing room without even checking on his brother's condition.

The Harts rallied to win the match. Afterward, as Keith, Bruce, and Bret celebrated, Owen stormed back to the ring, pushed Bret to the mat and screamed, "I don't need you!"

Stu and Helen couldn't believe what they were seeing. Bret couldn't believe what had happened. Stu tried to intervene, but Owen wouldn't be reasoned with.

"Why do those guys always have to get in the way?" Owen asked his father. "I never get any recognition!"

Owen didn't show up for Thanksgiving dinner. The Hart family was in turmoil.

Who Is the King of Harts?

S tu and Helen Hart tried desperately to keep their family together. The last thing they wanted was to see their sons at odds with each other in the ring. For a while, it looked as though the differences between Bret and Owen were only temporary. They even formed a tag team and wrestled WWF world tag team champions the Quebecers at the 1994 Royal Rumble.

But that match led to more trouble. When Bret refused to tag in, despite having suffered a leg injury earlier in the match, and the brothers lost the match, Owen was enraged.

"Why didn't you tag me?" Owen demanded. "I knew your leg was hurt, but all you had to do was tag me! But no, you're too damn selfish!"

Owen, it seemed, was tired of being overshadowed by his older brother. Bret had achieved superstardom. Owen was struggling to gain a foothold in the top ranks of the WWF. Of course, Bret was older than Owen and had been wrestling longer, but that didn't mean much to Owen, who allowed his jealousy to get the best of him.

The result was the brother's continuing battle being named 1994's Feud of the Year, as picked by the readers of *Pro Wrestling Illustrated* magazine.

At WrestleMania X on March 20, 1994, at Madison Square Garden in New York, Owen punished his brother's injured left leg as if he was trying to cripple him. He showed absolutely no regard for the welfare of his brother. His reward: a stunning pinfall victory after twenty minutes of brutal warfare.

Owen couldn't seem to poke his head out of Bret's shadow, even on this night. Bret had one more match to wrestle that evening, against WWF world champion Yokozuna. Although Bret limped to the ring for the WrestleMania main event, he took advantage of a mistake by the 500-pound Sumo wrestler to score the pin and become a two-time WWF world champion.

Naturally, that enraged Owen even further. At the 1994 King of the Ring, Owen had Jim Neidhart—Bret's former partner—help him beat Razor Ramon in the King of the Ring final. Bret was stunned by Neidhart's deception. As for Owen, he let everybody know, "I'm the King of the Ring!"

"The War Between the Harts" raged on. They met again at SummerSlam '94 in Chicago, where Davey Boy Smith entered the feud on Bret's behalf. But perhaps the most incredible incident of this feud occurred at the 1994 Survivor Series on

November 23 in San Antonio, Texas. Davey Boy was in Bret's corner for a WWF world title defense against Bob Backlund. Owen was in Backlund's corner. In this submission match, both corner men held a white towel. They were to throw in the towel if their man wanted to submit.

After Davey Boy was knocked out late in the match, Backlund applied his "chicken wing." The chicken wing, a variation of the sharpshooter, is an excruciatingly painful leglock. Sweat poured down Bret's face as he desperately tried to break the hold. Stu and Helen Hart, sitting at ringside, watched in horror as Bret howled in pain. Owen, watching from Backlund's corner, suddenly screamed, "I'm sorry!"

Bret Hart's feud with his own brother took its toll on his career and on his family life.

Was Owen trying to make up with Bret? Had he finally realized how much damage this family feud was causing? Owen begged his mother to throw in the towel. As tears streamed down her face, she agreed. She got up from her seat, walked to the ring, grabbed the towel, and threw it into the ring. The referee called for the bell. Bret had lost the belt.

Owen laughed! He had fooled his own mother.

This should have been a great time in Bret's life. He was a bigger star than ever, and he had even appeared on several episodes of the television show *Lonesome Dove*. He and National Hockey League stars Theo Fleury and Joe

Sakic also founded the Calgary Hitmen, a junior hockey team.

In the ring, however, everything went wrong for Bret. He received few title shots, having instead decided to concentrate on feuds with his brother and Jerry Lawler. For nearly a year, Bret was merely on the fringes of the WWF world championship.

Finally, Bret got his chance to regain the gold at the 1995 Survivor Series in Landover, Maryland. His opponent was Diesel, a seven-foot-tall monster who weighed 356 pounds (Diesel now wrestles as Kevin Nash in WCW). In an amazing display of perseverance, Bret rallied after Diesel smashed him through the announcers' table and scored the pin at

24:42. Bret was the WWF's second three-time world champion.

Rather than turning up his schedule as he had after his previous world title victories, Bret cut back. And after losing to Shawn Michaels in 1996's Match of the Year at WrestleMania XIII, Bret announced that he was going home to spend more time with his wife, Julie, and their four children.

From his home in Calgary, Bret took a look at himself and thought long and hard about the wrestling world—how it was changing and how the so-called bad guys were ruling wrestling. Fans were rooting for men like Michaels and Stone Cold Steve Austin, whose rebel behavior would have made them rulebreakers in the past. Bret did not like what he was seeing.

There was no way Bret was going to cater to the fans' whims. He wasn't going to flip off his opponents, shout obscenities, get drunk, and become lewd and crude. When he returned to the ring in late 1996, he continued to be the man he always was: hardworking, tough, and proud. He couldn't understand why the fans in the United States didn't seem to like him anymore.

Not that it stopped him from being the best that he could be. At In Your House XIII on February 16, 1997, in Chattanooga, Tennessee, Bret won a four-way match against Austin, the Undertaker, and Big Van Vader for his fourth WWF world title.

"This victory is for me," Bret told *Pro Wrestling Illustrated Weekly.* "I proved that I'm still the best that there is, and I'll prove it in the ring every night if I have to."

One night later, Austin's interference caused Bret to lose the world title to Sid Vicious. When Bret complained about Austin's actions, he found out exactly how the new breed of wrestling fans judged their heroes: Fans booed Bret because they thought he was a whiner.

As the world went topsy-turvy around him, Bret struggled for ways to understand what was going on. After losing again to Vicious, this time because of the Undertaker's interference, Bret slammed WWF owner Vince McMahon to the mat.

When Bret beat Austin in a submission match at WrestleMania XIII, the boos got louder. Bret was in shock. He couldn't believe that the fans had betrayed him. They were rooting for Austin, the bad guy—the man who drank beer on TV and cursed during his interviews. And they were rooting against him, the good guy who had tried to be a positive role model.

Bret's anger came to a head during the WWF's weekly *Raw* telecast on March 24, 1997, when he told the fans exactly what he thought about them.

"You take a gutless creep like Stone Cold Steve Austin, and beat him to a bloody pulp even though he knows, and you all know, that he lost," Bret said. "You cheer him on the way back to the dressing room like he won. It didn't just start right here. You cheered on a pretty boy like Shawn Michaels and you allowed him to screw me out of the WWF championship belt. I find myself sitting at home, watching the WWF on TV in Calgary, saying to myself, 'The WWF needs a hero. They need a role model, somebody they can look up to. Not somebody that's got earrings all over himself and tattoos ... not somebody who poses for girlie magazines.'"

As Bret spoke, the fans chanted Austin's name.

Though Bret was still a hero in Canada, he had become one of the most hated men in the United States. The good news was that Bret's war with the American fans ended his feud with Owen. The brothers teamed with Davey Boy Smith to form the New Hart Foundation. Brian Pillman and Jim Neidhart also joined the Foundation.

Bret won his fifth and finaL WWF world title at SummerSlam '97 in East Rutherford, New Jersey. He beat the Undertaker after special referee Shawn Michaels had mistakenly hit the Undertaker with a chair. He was trying to hit Bret. Boos rained down from the fans in the Meadowlands Arena as Bret strapped the belt around his waist.

It would be nice to say that Bret was elated after becoming the federation's first five-time world champion, but he wasn't. Weeks later, Bret received a phone call from Vince McMahon, who told him the federation could no longer afford his twenty-year contract. McMahon urged Bret to look elsewhere, so that's what he did. He contacted WCW, which had offered him a three-year, $9 million contract the year before. Bret and WCW quickly reached an agreement.

Bret's final match in the WWF was at the Survivor Series on November 9, 1997, in Montreal. His opponent was Shawn Michaels. Bret was looking forward to his match. His wife and kids would be there, and the Canadian fans would be on his side. Bret hoped to beat

Michaels, end his WWF run as world champion, and then hand back the belt. All that was wishful thinking.

Unfortunately, McMahon wanted Bret to lose on purpose. Bret refused. Late in the match, Michaels placed Bret in a sharpshooter. Three seconds later, the referee called for the bell and announced that Bret had submitted. Bret hadn't submitted, of course, but he knew immediately that McMahon had deceived him. That night, he stormed out of the ring, found McMahon, and beat him to a pulp.

And then Bret moved on.

The Final Stop

If Bret Hart had any plans to make amends with the fans and start over in WCW, those plans quickly went awry. If Hart had any plans to mend fences with the U.S. fans who hated him, then those plans were never apparent. For several years, Bret Hart had been the man in Canada, and the hated man in the United States.

Hart's first move was for the good guys: He helped Sting win the WCW world title from Hulk Hogan at Starrcade '97 in

Washington, DC. But on the Monday *Nitro* TV show on April 20, 1998, in Colorado Springs, Colorado, Hart's interference helped Hogan regain the belt from Randy Savage. The wrestling world was shocked: Hart had sided with the New World Order, the most notorious clique in wrestling. This was shocking for several reasons, but mostly because Hart had detested Hogan in the WWF. The two men couldn't have been more different.

Hart and Hogan teamed to beat Roddy Piper and Savage at the 1998 Great American Bash in Atlanta. Hart forced Savage to submit to his sharpshooter. But the fans were seeing a different side of the Hitman. He used a foreign object to beat

Chris Benoit. He slammed Booker T over the head with a chair.

No doubt about it: Hart was breaking the rules. On July 20, 1998, in Salt Lake City, Utah, Hart was scheduled to wrestle Diamond Dallas Page for the vacant U.S. title. Hart had Hogan attack Page early in the show. When the time came for the match against Hart, Page limped to the ring. He was no match for Hart's sharpshooter. The Hitman had his first title in WCW. Three weeks later, he lost the title to Lex Luger in a brass knuckles match. Three days after that, Hart regained the belt from Luger.

Hart didn't really have any friends in the WCW. His relationship with Hogan crashed when the Hulkster hit Hart with a

Hart delivers a punishing reverse suplex to an opponent.

foreign object. Although Hart had never officially joined the NWO, he was enraged by Hogan's deception . . . or so it seemed. Weeks later, Hogan and Hart brutally attacked Sting and embraced after they had done their dirty deed.

Hart's month reign as U.S. champion ended on October 26, 1998, in Phoenix, Arizona, when he lost to Diamond Dallas Page. Hart and WWF fan favorite Page hated each other. At World War III, Hart used a DDT, a Russian legsweep, and a figure-four leglock on Page. Page countered with a sharpshooter and his Diamond cutter to regain the U.S. title. But the relentless Hart recaptured the title from Page on November 30, 1998, in Chattanooga, Tennessee.

The Hitman grimaces as he traps Booker T in a headlock.

Hart's relationship with the U.S. fans deteriorated, as did their respect for him. He was widely criticized for not putting his U.S. title on the line in several matches against Sting. Sting won all of those matches, causing the Hitman to gloat, "He's a d--- good wrestler when there's no pressure." Piper, not Sting, beat Hart for the U.S. title on February 8, 1999, in Buffalo, New York.

Over the following weeks, Hart campaigned WCW officials for shots at the WCW world title. He was turned down. On March 29, 1999, a sellout crowd packed the Air Canada Centre in Toronto for the first-ever *Nitro* broadcast in Canada.

"We want Bret! We want Bret!" the crowd chanted. The words were like music to Hart's ears. He hadn't been cheered like this since he had joined WCW. During the card, Hart complained to WCW announcer Gene Okerlund about being overlooked for title shots and he challenged former WCW world champion Bill Goldberg. Suddenly, Goldberg stormed the ring and speared Hart in the chest. But after the spear, both men lay motionless on the

Sting drags Hart by his hair during one of their fiercely contested bouts.

mat for several minutes. After a few minutes, Hart rolled over onto Goldberg and covered him for the pin. Hart then removed his Toronto Maple Leafs jersey, revealing a metal vest.

"I quit!" he announced to the fans.

"I proved I'm still the best," Hart said afterward. "I beat the top guy they had, and in such a clever way. I would have liked to have left on a nicer note, but any kind of good-bye to all my fans would be hard, and WCW would probably cut to a commercial anyway."

Hart went home to Calgary. He seriously thought that his career was over. There was no way he could ever go back to the WWF, not after what had happened in his final match against Shawn Michaels. He didn't think he was getting a fair break in WCW. Then tragedy struck.

On May 23, 1999, Owen Hart died of cardiac arrest after plummeting more than fifty feet to the ring before a match at Kemper Arena in Kansas City, Missouri. The death of his beloved younger brother at Kemper Arena left Bret struggling for words and for a way to deal with this tragedy.

"The important thing I take pride in is knowing that they really recognized him for what he was. He was a great human being," Hart said on CNN's *Larry King Live*. "It wasn't so much the recognition for being a wrestler, but he was a great wrestler, too."

Hart returned to the ring late that summer and had several matches. On October 4, 1999, he wrestled Chris Benoit at Kemper Arena, the same building in which Owen had died. After Hart won this emotional match by locking Benoit in the sharpshooter, both men hugged and saluted Owen.

Hart had returned to action for a reason: to win the WCW world title. He got his shot when the world title was put up for grabs in a thirty-two-man tournament. The final two rounds were held at the Air Canada Centre, the same arena in which Hart had announced his retirement earlier in the year. Hart beat Sting to earn a spot in the finals. His opponent was Chris Benoit.

Bret Hart's match that night will be remembered. He used his sharpshooter to beat Benoit and became the fifth man in history to win both the WWF and WCW world titles. The others are Hulk Hogan, Kevin Nash, Ric Flair, and Randy Savage.

The fans were always seeing two sides of Bret Hart. Bret Hart the gentleman surfaced on December 26, when he scored a controversial victory in a title defense against Bill Goldberg. Hart offered to give up the title. But the next night at Starrcade '99 in a rematch against Goldberg, the Hitman had Goldberg caught in a sharp-shooter for only a few seconds when referee Roddy Piper called for the bell. Of course, Goldberg hadn't really submitted.

The match was reminiscent of what had happened to Hart at the 1997 Survivor Series, but in reverse.

But in mid-January, a concussion once again forced Hart to the sidelines. He was ordered to vacate the belt. Apparently, the injury had occurred in a match on December 21, 1999, against Goldberg in Washington, DC. Hart was kicked in the head during the match.

The truth was that Owen's death had made Bret think twice about his profession. He had always loved to wrestle, but his brother's death made him realize that he didn't love it enough to risk his life. His wife, children, and family came first. At forty-two years of age, having enjoyed a

Bret Hart helped professional wrestling evolve into a multimillion dollar, worldwide phenomenon.

lucrative, successful ring career, the Hitman had nothing more to prove. Finally, in late October 2000, Bret Hart officially retired.

"We are never prepared for what we expect," he said. "After great deliberation it has become clear that it is best for me, my family, and my fans that I say good-bye. Wrestling has been my life forever. I have been extremely fortunate in what I have achieved and what I have attained through wrestling. Wrestling will always be in my blood."

For a while, he was the best there was. And although you could argue forever about whether he's the best there ever will be, his record speaks for itself. Bret "the Hitman" Hart is a wrestling legend.

Glossary

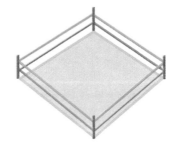

brass knuckles match   Special type of match in which both wrestlers wear brass knuckles on their hands.

clique   Small, exclusive group of people; for example, in pro wrestling, the New World Order and the Four Horsemen.

clothesline   Offensive move in which the attacker sticks out his or her arm and strikes his or her opponent across the throat.

Crippler crossface   Type of submission hold that puts pressure on the opponent's head and neck.

DDT   Offensive maneuver in which the attacker grabs the opponent in a facelock, wraps one arm around the opponent's neck, then drops to the mat, sending the victim's head into the canvas.

disqualification   Ruling by the referee in which a wrestler automatically loses a match for violating a rule.

draw   In wrestling, a match in which neither wrestler wins. A tie.

feud   Series of matches between two wrestlers or two tag teams. Frequently, one wrestler will badmouth the other wrestler or will sneak attack the wrestler.

figure-four leglock Submission move in which the attacker wraps his leg around and inside his opponent's legs and applies pressure on the thighs and lower back.

flying axhandle Offensive move in which the attacker mounts the ropes, locks his or her hands together, leaps, and brings his or her locked hands down upon the opponent.

foreign object Illegal object used in the ring, such as a chair or a pencil.

main event The featured match at a wrestling show, usually the last match of the night.

neckbreaker Offensive move in which the attacker wraps his or her arm around the opponent's neck and yanks him or her to the mat.

pin When either both shoulders or both shoulder blades are held in contact with the mat for three continuous seconds. A pin ends a match.

pinfall Win achieved by a pin.

rulebreaker In wrestling, a bad character, often someone disliked by the fans. So-called because he or she violates the rulebook.

scientific match Match between two or more wrestlers in which the combatants rely mostly on amateur wrestling moves, rather than kicking and punching.

sharpshooter   Type of submission hold.

sleeper   Finishing move in which the attacker wraps one arm around the opponent's neck and one arm around the opponent's forehead, placing pressure on the brain and causing the opponent to pass out.

small package   Counter-wrestling move in which the wrestler being pinned grabs the opponent's legs or upper body, rolls him or her over, and places him or her into pinning position.

submission hold   Wrestling move that makes an opponent give up without being pinned.

submission match Special match in which the only way to win is by forcing your opponent to submit.

submits Wrestler's decision to give in to an opponent's finishing maneuver. A submission ends the match.

suplex When a wrestler picks up his or her opponent and drops them backward to the ground, all the while holding on.

tag team match Match involving two teams of two or more wrestlers. Only one wrestler from each team is allowed in the ring at a time.

technical wrestlers Professional wrestlers who use basic amateur wrestling moves and try to win matches by outthinking and out-wrestling their opponents, rather than wearing them down with kicks and punches.

vertical suplex Offensive move in which the attacker lifts the opponent, turns him or her upside-down, then falls backward so that the opponent's back and head smash against the mat.

For More Information

Magazines

Pro Wrestling Illustrated, The Wrestler, Inside Wrestling, Wrestle America, and *Wrestling Superstars*
London Publishing Co.
7002 West Butler Pike
Ambler, PA 19002

WCW Magazine
P.O. Box 420235
Palm Coast, FL 32142-0235

WOW Magazine

McMillen Communications

P.O. Box 500

Missouri City, TX 77459-9904

e-mail: woworder@mcmillencomm.com

Web Sites

Professional Wrestling Online Museum

http://www.wrestlingmuseum.com

Pro Wrestling Torch

http://www.pwtorch.com

World Championship Wrestling

http://www.wcw.com

World Wrestling Federation

http://www.wwf.com

For Further Reading

Albano, Lou, Bert Randolph Sugar, and
Michael Benson. *The Complete
Idiot's Guide to Pro Wrestling.*
2nd ed. New York: Alpha Books, 2000.

Archer, Jeff. *Theater in a Squared
Circle.* New York: White-Boucke
Publishing, 1998.

Cohen, Dan. *Wrestling Renegades:
An In-Depth Look at Today's*

Superstars of Pro Wrestling.
New York: Archway, 1999.

Hofstede, David. *Slammin':
Wrestling's Greatest
Heroes and Villains.*
New York: ECW Press, 1999.

Mazer, Sharon. *Professional
Wrestling: Sport and Spectacle.*
Jackson, MS: University Press
of Mississippi, 1998.

Myers, Robert. *The Professional
Wrestling Trivia Book.* Boston,
MA: Branden Books, 1999.

Works Cited

Burkett, Harry. "Bret Hart Gets A Title Gift From Shawn Michaels." *The Wrestler Digest*, Spring, 1998, pp. 42–47.

Hart, Bret. *Bret "Hitman" Hart: The Best There Is, the Best There Was, the Best There Ever Will Be.* New York: Stoddart, 2000.

"Press Conference: Bret Hart." *Pro Wrestling Illustrated*, November, 1998, pp. 22–23.

Rodriguez, Andy. "Bret Hart: Cheating Himself Out of Respect." *The Wrestler*, January, 1999, pp. 38–41.

Rosenbaum, Dave. "Bret Screws Bret, Part II." *Pro Wrestling Illustrated*, October, 1998, pp. 26–30.

Index

Photo Credits

All photos © Colin Bowman.

Series Design and Layout

Geri Giordano